DOC' WILLIAM PALMER

THE RUGELEY POISONER

By

JOHN GODWIN

© John Godwin
ISBN 0 9515913 1 2

CONTENTS

	Page
Introduction	3
Chapter 1 Early Days	5
Chapter 2 More Strange Deaths	12
Chapter 3 Insurance Money to the Rescue	16
Chapter 4 The Law catches up with Palmer	21
Chapter 5 The Trial and Imprisonment of Palmer	29
Chapter 6 The Day of Reckoning	35

INTRODUCTION

The trial of Dr William Palmer of Rugeley ranks as one of the most famous of the nineteenth century. All the evidence surrounding the case was circumstantial, and there are those who believe that Palmer would not have been found guilty if he had been tried today. There is no doubt whatever that he was a rogue, a forger, and a man of immoral character, and in my opinion he was also a murderer. However, it could be that some crimes were attributed to him by people who were only too keen to "give a dog a bad name", once he had embarked upon his wayward life.

This account of the Palmer story (greatly shortened, for the sake of clarity) does not attempt to speculate on which stories might be true, and which might not. It attempts merely to summarise the alleged crimes of the man from contemporary accounts, and to tell them in the way that they were believed to have happened by the man in the street at the time of Dr Palmer. Readers are urged to delve more fully into the story (there is ample coverage of the trial in the press of the day) before drawing their own conclusions.

There are still a number of tangible reminders of Palmer in the streets of Rugeley. His house still stands, though it is now shops. The Talbot Arms Inn (now the Shrew Kafé Bar) is still to be seen opposite the house. Mrs Palmer Senior's house is to be found almost opposite St Augustine's Church, while the Palmer family grave is located at the rear of the Church. The grave of John Parsons Cook is not far from the entrance to the Parish Church.

So infamous was Palmer in his day that he was featured in the Chamber of Horrors in Madame Tussaud's Waxworks in London from 1857 to 1979. This year, a special "200 Years" exhibition has been opened at the Museum, and there is on display there a watercolour portrait of Palmer as a young man, together with a box containing some bottles of poison which belonged to him.

Palmer's trial had widespread social implications. The proceedings were very widely reported in great detail, and there was an enormous surge of popular interest. Nineteenth century society existed largely on the basis of a secure, fixed and eternal order of things, but the doubts engendered by the medical evidence presented at the trial, and by the exposures revealed in the private life of a medical man in a small provincial town, seemed to have a deep impact on Victorian life and values. Further, the public hanging of Palmer, as reported by the press, was for many people almost a festive occasion, and it must have been obvious to many in authority that the main purpose of a public execution - that of a deterrent to others - was hardly to the fore. Public hangings were employed for twelve more years, but the end was in sight.

My thanks are due to the Trustees of the William Salt Library at Stafford for access to old copies of the Staffordshire Advertiser, for permission to reproduce the 'Jane' letter, and (jointly with Shugborough County Museum) for permission to photograph and reproduce the death mask of William Palmer. My special thanks are also due to Mr Don Brown of Cannock Library for reading my script, and to my wife and son for invaluable help.

Rugeley, Staffs.   John Godwin.
1992.

Chapter 1
Early Days

William Palmer was born in the large house in Station Road, Rugeley, next to the Old Chancel. He was christened in St Augustine's Church on Oct. 21st., 1824.

His maternal grandfather was said to have stolen a considerable sum of money from a lady who ran a brothel in Derby, and to have moved later to King's Bromley. His daughter (Palmer's mother) was courted by the Steward of the Marquis of Anglesey, and also by Dr Palmer's father, Joseph, a Sawyer. She married Joseph Palmer, though the Steward continued to pay her attention, and while he was thus occupied Joseph was engaged in a "fiddle" with the Marquis's timber. In this way he made a lot of money, and moved to Station Road, Rugeley. His network of dishonesty also extended to the Bagot estate, where he increased his illegal gains. Unfortunately, he dropped dead suddenly at home in 1837 while enjoying his bread and cheese, and was buried in Rugeley churchyard. He left an unsigned Will, but it was agreed that the five sons should each have £7,000, and that the widow should keep the remainder, providing she did not marry again.

Although Mrs Palmer kept her promise not to remarry, she was never short of men-friends. One of her most ardent lovers was a Mr Duffy, twenty years her junior, who used to stay at the Shoulder of Mutton public house in Rugeley (situated where the clock belonging to the former Town Hall now stands). The landlord of the Shoulder of Mutton, Tom Clewley, remembered Duffy as a fine-looking man with white hair and a cherry-red face. Eventually Duffy left Rugeley without trace, leaving several cases of luggage behind. Clewley and his wife

The Shoulder of Mutton Inn

opened the cases, to reveal dirty laundry and also a series of amorous letters written by Mrs Palmer, in which she arranged to meet Duffy at various times for love-making. After Duffy's departure, his place in Mrs Palmer's affections was quickly filled by Mr Jerry Smith, a Rugeley Solicitor.

There were seven children in the Palmer family. Joseph, the eldest, was a wealthy merchant, living in Liverpool at the time Dr Palmer became notorious. Next came William; then George, a Rugeley Solicitor; then Walter, a chronic alcoholic; and finally Thomas, a Church of England Clergyman. There were also two daughters, the elder of whom drank herself to death, and the younger of whom was a charming and accomplished lady, liked by all.

The day after Palmer's birth in 1824, the grocer living near the house sent his apprentice to give his congratulations to the mother. This apprentice, Thomas Sidney by name, lived in Stafford and walked to Rugeley and back for his work. Later he became a very wealthy man through importing tea, and ultimately he occupied the position of Lord Mayor of London. While he was Alderman in London, he took his official place on the bench at the Central Criminal Court at the trial of William Palmer, the man whose mother he had congratulated all those years earlier!

It seems that while Mr Palmer Senior was alive, there was strict discipline in the Palmer household, but after his death the mother was no longer able to keep control of her family, and the discipline vanished.

William was a good-natured though sly young boy. He attended Rugeley Grammar School under Headmasters Clark and Bonney, and was probably a pupil there at the same time as Thomas George Bonney, son of the Headmaster, who became a world-famous geologist and

Dr William Palmer

who was elected President of the British Association in 1910. Palmer achieved something of a reputation at school for borrowing money from people in a plausible way, and then spending it indiscriminately.

After leaving school he went to Liverpool to be apprenticed to Evans and Evans, Wholesale Druggists. He seemed to have embarked upon his lascivious sexual career at this point, for he is reported to have seduced a girl while with the firm. He also displayed his dishonesty by intercepting money sent by post to his firm. An Inspector was sent to investigate, but the traps which were set yielded nothing. Eventually one of the partners caught Palmer opening one of the firm's letters, and sacked him. Mrs Palmer agreed to replace the stolen money, and to avoid complete family disgrace it was arranged for Palmer's brother to finish the apprenticeship.

Money stolen by Palmer at this time from his employers was spent in betting on the race-course, and also in keeping company with women of doubtful repute. Palmer's life, it seems, was now irrecovocably set on its course.

When he was eighteen he was apprenticed for five years to Dr Edward Tylecote, of Great Haywood, but his dishonesty soon asserted itself again. While attending a patient who had been tossed by a bull, Palmer asked the owner of the bull if he could change a £5 note. He accepted the five sovereigns, but fumbled in his pockets without finding the note. He promised to send it on later, but failed to do so. The money was eventually paid by Mrs Palmer. Often, instead of visiting local patients, he would call to see a local lady he had seduced. He once went with another of his lady friends, Jane Widnall, to Walsall, where his brothers found him and were forced to settle his debts. So keen was he to visit Jane at home that he would arrange to be

Palmer's mother's house

called out of a Church service (which he regularly attended), ostensibly to visit a patient, but in reality to visit Jane while her parents were still in Church. The deceit was discovered, and Palmer promised to marry the girl, but failed to do so.

His next job was at Stafford Infirmary, where he seems to have taken an extraordinary interest in the poisons in the Dispensary - so much so that a rule was introduced forbidding pupils to enter the room.

While he was employed at the Infirmary, we hear of Palmer allegedly attempting to poison a man named Abley in a local public house. He is supposed to have challenged Abley to a drinking bout, to a point where the man staggered outside and was sick in the stable. He later died there. The Foreman of the Jury at the Inquest was not happy with the "Death from Natural Causes" verdict. He was convinced that Palmer had poisoned Abley.

Towards the end of 1846, Palmer went to London to finish his medical training under one Dr. Stegall. He needed all the help he could get in his studies, and promised the doctor 50 guineas if he would "cram" him to pass the exams. Surprisingly, Palmer did pass his exams, but failed to pay Dr. Stegall.

Palmer's stay in London was marked by riotous behaviour, in his giving extravagant parties, in betting heavily, and in keeping company with low City women. His reputation while in London is perhaps best summarised by the attitude of a hospital official, who refused Palmer's request to let him lodge with him, on the grounds that he felt his daughters might be in moral danger by doing so.

Chapter 2
More Strange Deaths

Colonel Brookes, late Indian Army, lived in Stafford. He had had four brothers who had all committed suicide. He had never married, but made his housemaid, Miss Ann Thornton his mistress. She used her position to tyrannise the Colonel, and she became an alcoholic, being often found in a completely drunken state. Eventually the Colonel became so harassed that he shot himself. Their daughter Ann Brookes had been born in 1827, and she proved to be a kind, cheerful, engaging child. Under the Colonel's Will, he left his daughter and his mistress a considerable sum, but there were legal complications, as the result of which the daughter became a Ward in Chancery, under her guardian, Charles Dawson of Stafford, who had a country residence at Abbot's Bromley. Palmer used to go to Abbot's Bromley to court Ann Brookes when she was eighteen. By this time, Ann was very sensitive about her status as an illegitimate child, but Palmer, always a "charmer" with women, eventually won her over, in spite of warnings from Mr Dawson, who had heard of Palmer's reputation.

The couple were married at Abbot's Bromley Church on 7th October, 1847. Palmer had returned to Rugeley in the previous year after obtaining the Diploma of the Royal College of Surgeons. He followed his profession as a doctor from his house in Market Street, Rugeley (still standing), and on 11th October, 1848, the first child William, was born. He committed suicide in 1925, at the age of 77.

Four later children of the marriage all died in infancy. The family nurse, Ann Bradshaw, was convinced that Palmer had poisoned all of them. She

Dr Palmer's house (now shops)

ran into a public house after the death of the fourth, shouting that she would never enter the Palmer house again. Palmer had apparently sent her downstairs from the nursery, telling her that he would nurse the child for a time. Shortly afterwards, she heard cries, ran upstairs, and found that the child had died a few seconds earlier. One account said that Palmer killed his children by putting poison on his finger, then dusting it with sugar, then placing it in the babies' mouths to suck. Presumably the reason for these alleged killings was that Palmer found it impossible to pay for his children's upkeep.

It seems clear that Palmer did not have the determination to suceed as a doctor. His Rugeley practice gradually lapsed, and he felt drawn to ways of making money more quickly (as he thought) to pay for his wayward lifestyle. He had always been interested in horse-racing - Rugeley was noted for its annual horse fair in June - but he now became obsessed with it as a means of getting rich quickly. He had a stable on the outskirts of Rugeley, incorporating several of the adjacent fields, and he also had training facilities with a Hednesford trainer. He raced horses on many occasions, but was often suspected of dishonest racing practices.

In general, he lost heavily on horse racing, but always took his losses stoically, determined to make good next time. Word quickly spread that Palmer was a man who did not pay his debts, and he began to experience serious trouble with moneylenders.

Rumours about his impecunious state now began to multiply. A Rugeley woman, Jane Mumford, had an illegitimate child by Palmer, but he could not afford the upkeep of the child, so after seeing it on the pretext of verifying that it was still alive, he sent it home, but it died soon afterwards.

He approached his wife's mother to see if she would lend him money, but his initial efforts were to no avail. Eventually, the mother feared that her refusal to lend money might result in Palmer's ill-use of her daughter, so she lent him £20. He thanked her, and invited her to visit him and his wife. Reluctantly, she accepted, but died while staying with her daughter. Prophetically, she had said before leaving her own house, "I know I shall not live a fortnight". But Palmer did not benefit financially by her Will, as he had hoped to do.

Equally suspicious circumstances surrounded the death of Mr Bladon, from Ashby-de-la-Zouche, who visited Palmer in May 1850, to collect some money owed to him. In a short time he became very ill, and eventually Palmer, anxious not to take full responsibility for dealing with the illness, sent for his old colleague Dr Bamford of Rugeley, who was asked to prescribe something. Mrs Bladon arrived to see her husband soon afterwards. She wanted other relatives to visit the sick man, but Palmer made the excuse that the journey to Ashby and back would take too long, and would not be worth it. Bladon died, and was speedily buried. After his death, his widow commented on the small amount of money he had on his person, whereas she knew he had set out from Ashby with a considerable sum. Palmer tried to make Mrs Bladon sign a note to the effect that he was owed money by Bladon, whereas in reality it seems that the reverse was true.

The dead man's brother was highly suspicious of foul play, but Mrs Bladon did not wish to embarrass Mrs Palmer by any accusations against her husband, unless there was more evidence of a crime having been committed.

People's tongues were now wagging fast. They

recalled the deaths of Palmer's children, of Abley, of Palmer's wife's mother, and also of Joseph Bentley (brother of Mrs Palmer senior), who lived at Longdon Green, and later at Uttoxeter. Palmer went to stay with him, and encouraged his uncle to drink heavily. Next morning, Bentley was taken ill, and died three days later.

Ominous clouds were beginning to gather for Dr William Palmer.

Chapter 3
Insurance Money to the Rescue

The wife of another of Mrs Palmer senior's brothers complained of feeling unwell one day while on a visit to Dr and Mrs Palmer. The doctor gave her some pills, but before she took them she began to feel better. Palmer enquired next day how she was, and was upset to find that she had not taken his pills. He urged her to take them the following night, but feeling now quite fit, she decided to throw the pills out of the window. The poultry in the yard below swallowed them, and promptly died. This lady, Mrs Bentley, had been left some property by her father in law to help pay expenses in looking after her crippled husband, and it was conjectured that Palmer was trying to get his hands on the property by killing his aunt.

At about this time the Norfolk Chronicle reported that a Mr Bly, who was living near Beccles, had occasion to be attended by Palmer while at a race meeting. At the time of his illness, he had won a large sum of money from Palmer. When Bly's wife came to see how her husband was, Bly told her that Palmer owed him £800. Bly died shortly afterwards, and the wife applied to Palmer for the money. Palmer retorted that the sick man must have been deluded, for in reality it was Bly who owed Palmer the money. It seemed that this was yet another of

Palmer's poisonings.

After Colonel Brookes's death, it was discovered that by a flaw in the language of the Will, Palmer's wife had only a life interest in her share of the estate, and that after her death, the property would pass to the heir named in the Will. Palmer therefore saw no reason why he should not insure his wife for a substantial sum, so that when she died he would not lose everything. In attempting to obtain insurance cover for his wife, some companies declined the proposal, but eventually he obtained life cover for £13,000.

In September 1854, Palmer's wife went to a concert in Liverpool, and caught a chill. Next day she returned by train to Rugeley, and went straight to bed, still feeling unwell. Palmer took her up a cup of tea and some toast, which she ate, but vomited soon afterwards. To cover himself, Palmer invited 82-year-old Dr Bamford to see his wife, and he gave her some pills and some medicine. He called again two days later, to find only one pill had been taken. Shortly afterwards, poor Mrs Palmer died and Dr Bamford certified the cause of death to be "English Cholera". The certificate was also signed by Dr Knight, an old Stafford doctor; and a third medical man, Benjamin Thirlby, a close associate of Palmer, also saw Mrs Palmer. One possibly suspicious circumstance associated with Palmer's wife's death was that she had frequently been seen to take effervescing drinks given to her by her husband.

The doctor buried his wife in the family vault in Rugeley churchyard, and appeared to be greatly distressed, weeping profusely at the graveside. He was consoled that night by his housemaid, Eliza Tharme, who, exactly nine months later, gave birth to Palmer's illegitimate son. The baby was born in Palmer's house in June 1855 (the incident is recorded in his diary), but died on 13th December

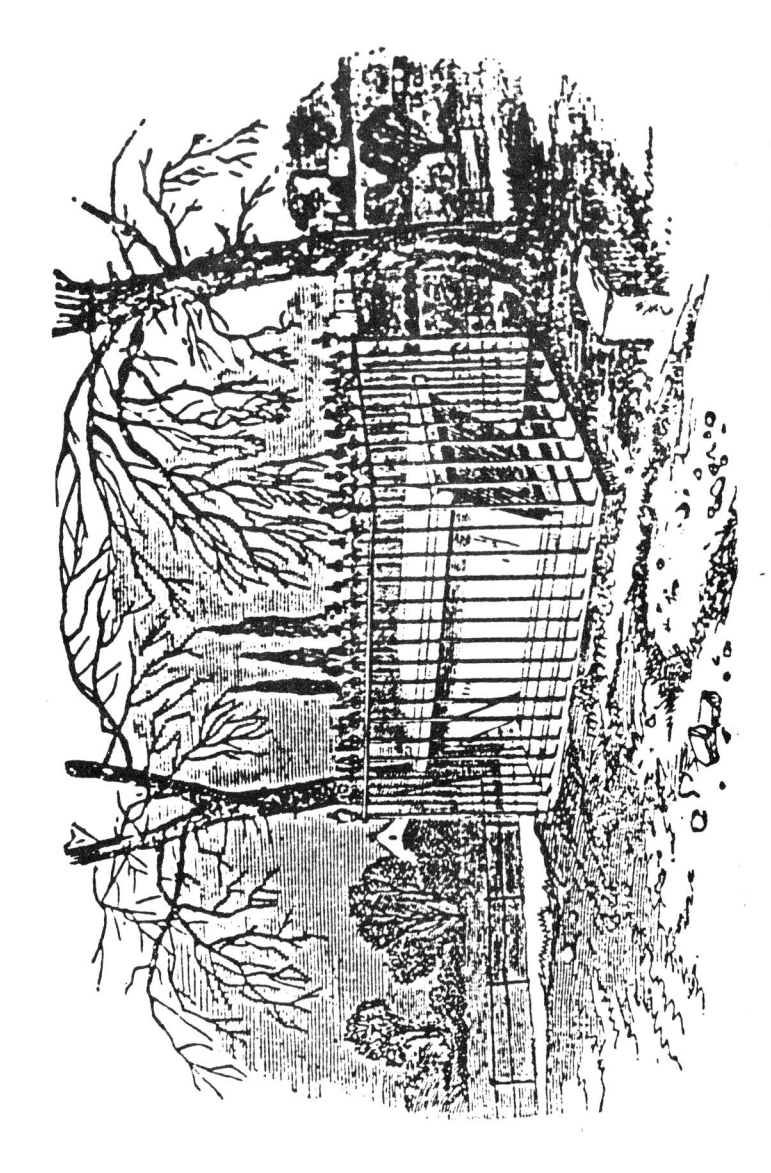

The Palmer family grave, St Augustine's Church, Rugeley, as it was last century

of the same year.

Palmer collected the insurance money from a suspicious company, and found a woman to look after his one remaining legitimate child. The money was soon gone in settlement of his many debts. To make ends meet, he now resorted to forging his mother's signature on bills, which he attempted to discount in London and elsewhere.

Many people thought that Palmer's wife, who had witnessed the deaths of most of her children and also of her mother, had a premonition of her own death. Eliza Tharme, a pretty girl of eighteen years, was the youngest of ten children of James and Mary Tharme of Colton. She often said that Palmer would have made advances to her before his wife's death, had she not been living in the same house as his wife. But there is no doubt that as soon as Mrs Palmer died, Eliza became one of his mistresses.

Palmer's brother Walter, an alcoholic, lived at Stafford. His wife was the daughter of a Liverpool ship builder, with a private income of £450 a year. Dr Palmer's eye fell on Walter as another candidate for an insurance policy, and he made proposals to six offices for sums totalling £82,000. The medical referee urged caution to the insurance companies, and the final amount of the insurance was much less than this. It is highly doubtful whether Palmer could have paid the premiums on the policies as originally conceived. Walter was as keen to go ahead with the insurance as Dr Palmer, as the doctor had promised to lend his brother a large sum of money as soon as the policy was effected.

Walter was often ill through excessive drinking, and at this point, perhaps somewhat conveniently, he became ill again, and went to bed at Stafford. It is said that at just this time, Dr Palmer was seen to buy prussic acid in Stafford, and he was seen making up a mixture in the Junction Hotel in that town. Whatever the sequence of events, Walter, who had spent the previous day at the races, suddenly took a turn for the worse, and died. Walter's wife was not at home at the time, and Dr Palmer saw that his brother was buried with what many thought to be undue haste in the family vault in Rugeley.

Walter's wife, unaware of her husband's illness, was given the news next day of her husband's death by William, who went to Liverpool to meet her. She expressed a wish to come to see Walter immediately, but William told her that in her absence he had made all the necessary funeral arrangements, and that in fact the body of her husband was already sealed in his coffin, though the interment had not yet taken place.

It transpired later that neither Walter nor his wife had known the amount for which his life had been insured, and at this stage Dr Palmer tried to get his sister-in-law to surrender any interest her late husband might have had in the policy. But in the event the insurance company refused to pay up, threatening to take Dr Palmer to court if he did not drop his claim.

It seems that Palmer still had not finished with life insurance, for he approached one George Bate with a proposal, hoping to make a handsome profit on the deal himself. But by now detectives from the insurance companies were on the trail, and some of the men they questioned would not reveal to Palmer the nature of the questions they had been asked, in spite of the doctor's persistence. One of the men questioned, Tom Myatt, vowed that the drink Palmer later offered him was laced with poison. The proposal on Bates's life was eventually refused.

Palmer was again in desperate financial straits. His chief moneylender and bill-discounter at this time seems to have been a Mr Pratt of London, but the rates of interest on the loans were extortionate. Somehow, Palmer must find a quick way to make more money.

Chapter 4
The Law catches up with Palmer

John Parsons Cook was a native of Lutterworth in Leicestershire. He had trained to be a Solicitor, but having a modest private income, he indulged in his favourite pastime, which was horse-racing. Cook was a pale, thin man, with long hair and a small moustache. Two or three rings were prominent on his fingers, and when out of doors he usually wore a loose-fitting overcoat. A good natured man, not given to excesses of temper, Cook had been on intimate terms with Palmer for some time. The doctor was now heavily in debt, and Cook also owed money. Palmer's money-making schemes had not succeeded of late, and in addition he was being blackmailed by a Stafford girl, thought by many to be Jane Bergen. She possessed a collection of indecent love letters written to her by Dr Palmer, and she threatened to show them to her father, a policeman, unless Palmer paid up. Palmer had persuaded Jane to have an operation to abort his child. The "Jane letters" are held at the County Record Office at Stafford, and they are noteworthy, amongst other things, for their sexual allusions. One letter. for example, reads as follows:

"My dear Jane, A lady asked me just how I liked last night's concert. I said, 'Very well', but I preferred a duet which followed! So I did - did you? Yours, W.P."

Cook owned racehorses, one of which, Polestar, was entered for the forthcoming Shrewsbury handicap. Polestar won, and Cook, profiting to the extent of £1,700, gave a dinner in celebration at the Raven

Dr Palmer's house on right, The Talbot Arms Inn on left. Rugeley Town Centre in the mid nineteenth century. Original Town Hall centre background

Hotel, Shrewsbury. Next day, Cook and Palmer were on the racecourse again. During that evening, Palmer was seen examining closely the contents of a tumbler of liquid, and later he was seen persuading Cook to have more to drink. Cook became violently ill, and gave a companion who was with him all his winnings, to guard. He later improved, and in spite of having suspected Palmer of poisoning his drink, it seems that the two men resumed their friendship and returned to Rugeley, where Cook booked a room at the Talbot Arms Hotel, exactly opposite Palmer's house. The Hotel was later re-named the Shrewsbury Arms, and in recent times it has become the Shrew Kafé Bar.

Next day, Cook was still feeling well, and dined at Palmer's house, but the next morning he was violently sick. Palmer sent him up some broth, which Cook vomited. The doctor attended Cook closely all that day, but the patient brought back everything the doctor gave him. Dr Bamford called in and left some pills. More broth was sent by Palmer, but the chambermaid, thinking it looked and smelt good, tasted it, and vomited violently.

Palmer decided to send a note to Cook's friend, Mr Jones of Lutterworth, asking him to come and see the patient. Next morning, Cook felt better, but Palmer dashed up to London with the intention of dealing fraudulently with Cook's money. When Palmer returned to Rugeley, he called at the Chemist's to obtain three grains of strychnine. On the same night he took Cook some pills, which made him very ill. Palmer insisted that the patient take two more pills, together with a dark-coloured liquid. Cook vomited again. Next day, Palmer purchased six grains of strychnine and two drams of prussic acid. In the afternoon, Mr Jones arrived from Lutterworth. Drs Palmer and Bamford jointly prepared more pills, and Palmer particularly asked Dr Bamford to write the instructions on the pill box. Later, Palmer administered two of the pills,

Mr Stephens

commenting to Mr Jones on how beautiful was Dr Bamford's writing on the box!

Mr Jones slept in the same room as Cook, but shortly after midnight Cook awoke in great pain, and sent Mr Jones for Dr Palmer. Palmer gave Cook two more pills.

A terrible scene now unfolded. In the words of a contemporary account, "Wildly shrieking, the patient tossed about in fearful convulsions; his limbs were so rigid that it was impossible to raise him, though he entreated that they would do so, as he felt that he was now suffocating. Every muscle was now convulsed, his body bent upwards like a bow. They turned him over on his left side; the action of the heart gradually ceased, and he was dead".

Palmer, who had already appropriated some of Cook's race-winnings, arranged for the deceased's body to be laid out quickly, and while this was being done he rummaged through the dead man's possessions to take away anything which might prove how much Cook had won.

A short time later, Cook's stepfather, Mr Stephens, having just heard of his stepson's death, came to Rugeley and questioned Dr Palmer about the circumstances. He was at once suspicious of Palmer, and when important papers of Cook's were found to be missing, he became even more suspicious.

Palmer endeavoured to obtain old Dr Bamford's signature on the death certificate, on which was entered "apoplexy" as the cause of death. At the post-mortem examination, Cook's intestines and stomach were found to be in a healthy condition, whereupon Palmer remarked to Dr Bamford, "They won't hang us yet!" There had been a suggestion that Cook had a syphilitic condition, but there was no proof of this.

Went to London to
pay Pratt — 7 00

Ret'd home by Fly
from Stafford —
Sat up with Cook all night

— 20 TUESDAY [324-41] —

Attending on Cook all day

dined at the Yard —

up with Cook all night

— 21 WEDNESDAY [325-40] —

xxx Cook died at 1 o'Clock
this morning

Jere & W'm Saunders
dined

Sent Bright a 3 mos Bill

Palmer's diary recording death of Cook

While the stomach and intestines were being placed in a jar, Palmer pushed against the man doing the work, almost upsetting the jar. Palmer then moved the jar to another part of the room without telling anyone, and it seemed quite obvious from his attitude that he was nervous about what a future examination of the contents might reveal.

Mr Stephens insisted that the contents of the jar be sent away for analysis, and he engaged a fly to take the jar to Stafford station, intending to take it from there to London himself. Palmer offered the driver £10 to upset the vehicle and its contents - surely an incriminating act -, but the bribe was refused. That evening, Palmer was said to be drunk as he reeled through the streets of Rugeley.

So anxious was Palmer to discover what the analysis of Cook's organs might reveal, that he bribed the Rugeley Postmaster, Mr Cheshire, to open any letter from London which might contain the result, and to let him know the verdict. A letter from London to the Rugeley Solicitor, intercepted by Cheshire, stated that no poison had been found. Palmer was obviously relieved. "I knew it", he said, "I'm as innocent as a baby".

Now Palmer tried to bribe the Coroner by sending him gifts of poultry, and he even hinted that the verdict should be that Cook "died of natural causes". The doctor who had conducted the analysis was suspicious, in spite of discovering nothing positive by way of poison in Cook's body. The fact that Palmer had bought strychnine only a day before Cook's death added to the suspicion. The Coroner's Jury returned a verdict of Wilful Murder, and Palmer was arrested, although he could not be removed immediately, as he was ill in bed.

Cook was eventually buried in St Augustine's churchyard, on Station Rd., Rugeley. One may see

Grave of John Parsons Cook in Rugeley Churchyard

the grave to the right as one passes through the gateway to the present Church. The inscription is still plainly decipherable, though it has been renovated since the original burial.

A few days after Palmer's arrest, the bodies of Ann Palmer (Palmer's wife) and Walter Palmer (his brother) were exhumed and viewed by a Jury. The post-mortem examinations were done by a Dr Alfred Taylor, of Guy's Hospital, London. Walter Palmer's cheeks were so swollen "as to extend to either side of the coffin; one eye was open, and the mouth partially so, presenting the appearance of a horrible grin and grimace". The arms and legs were terribly swollen, and several of the Jury were sick at the sight. The smell was indescribable, and the walls of the room had to be re-papered and the floor planed to get rid of the stench. Mrs Palmer's body was not swollen, the corpse being drier than Walter's.

The Inquest on the two bodies followed shortly afterwards. The verdict on Ann Palmer was that she had been killed by antimony poisoning, but that on Walter was not as conclusive. These cases were not proceeded with, however, because Palmer was to be tried for the murder of Cook.

Chapter 5
The Trial and Imprisonment of Palmer

Palmer was tried at the Central Criminal Court in London, rather than at Stafford Assizes. It was felt that local prejudice against him was very strong, so the Lord Chancellor introduced a Bill in the House of Lords to empower the Queen's Bench to order certain offenders to be tried away from the scene of their alleged crimes. The Bill (often referred to as the Palmer Act) received Royal assent on 11th April, 1856. So it was that Palmer was tried in London, rather than Stafford. The Bill is still on the Statute Book.

The trial was, by any standard, a sensational one, and lasted twelve days. Many of the most eminent medical men in the country were called to give evidence. It was not known at the time, of course, that one member of the Crown Counsel (also an M.P.) would himself be the centre of a scandal a few years later, when found guilty of fraud. He had fled to America to avoid the consequences of his actions.

This was the first trial in this country involving strychnine poisoning, and knowledge about its effects on the body was limited. Although no strychnine had been found on Cook's body, the prosecution case rested on the belief that because the symptoms associated with Cook's death resembled closely the known symptoms of death by strychnine, he could not have died of anything else. The Prosecution statement at the trial included the following:

"Now the way in which strychnine acting upon the voluntary muscles is fatal to life is that it produces the most intense excitement of all these muscles. Violent convulsions take place - spasms which affect the whole body, and which end in rigidity -, all the muscles become fixed; and the respiratory muscles in which the lungs have play are fixed with immovovable rigidity. Respiration consequently is suspended, and death ensues. Those symptoms are known to medical science under the name of tetanus" (This was an erroneous statement - seizures from strychnine do not come under the name of tetanus). "There are other forms of tetanus which produce death, and which arise from other causes than the taking of strychnine, but there is a wide difference between the various forms of the same disease, which prevents the possibility of mistake".

Palmer in the dock, Central Criminal Court

There is no doubt that Palmer's recent purchase of strychnine added considerable weight to the Prosecution's case.

There were divergences of medical opinion in the trial, and the whole proceedings were followed closely by the whole nation. But, Sir Benjamin Brodie, President of the Royal College of Surgeons, a man held in the highest esteem, gave it as his opinion that the way Cook died bore no relationship to any natural disease, and the indications pointed, without doubt, to death from strychnine. Eventually, Palmer was found guilty, and the Judge, Lord Chief Justice Campbell, wearing the black coif symbolic of the death penalty, sentenced Palmer to be hanged in his own County Town of Stafford.

He was transferred to Stafford gaol, in readiness for his public execution, which was planned for Saturday, June 14th., 1856, at 8.0 a.m. Contrary to popular local belief, this was not the last public hanging to take place in this country. The last public execution took place on May 26th., 1868, twelve years after Palmer.

Palmer repeatedly refused to confess his guilt, and attempted to starve himself in order to try to draw other people's attention to the injustice, as he saw it. In desperation the prison authorities threatened to force-feed him.

Before the day fixed for the execution, last-minute attempts for a reprieve had been made by Palmer's clergyman brother. Booklets were written by him, stressing the dangers of convicting a man entirely on circumstantial evidence, but to no avail.

On the last evening of his life, Palmer had several visitors in his cell. Two of his brothers and other members of his family came late at night. All hope of reprieve seemed now to have gone. Palmer seemed serene, except for the slight twitching of the muscles at the corner of his mouth, and that restless play of fingers which often seemed to occur involuntarily at his trial. When the members of his family had gone, the prisoner took brandy and water, and at 1.0 a.m. he retired to rest, sleeping until 2.30 a.m. He was roused to prepare himself for the visit of the Prison chaplain, who remained with him until 5.0 a.m., urging him to confess his guilt. He came again from 6.30 a.m. to 7.30 a.m. on the same mission. Palmer listened calmly, after which he asserted categorically that John Parsons Cook did not die from strychnine poisoning.

Another clergyman visited the prisoner at about 6.0 a.m. Palmer asked him whether a sinner could be saved by confessing his sins to God, without confessing them to man. The clergyman replied that he couldn't give an answer in the negative, as this might appear to limit the grace of God. After further thought, he added, "Your Bible tells you that all liars shall have their part in the lake of fire and brimstone. If you are guilty and yet continue to protest, you will go into Eternity with a lie upon your lips, and you know the consequences of that". The prisoner appeared moved, but said nothing.

Palmer presented his Solicitor, Jerry Smith, with a book entitled "The Sinner's Friend", in which he wrote, "The gift of William Palmer, June 13th., 1856". A little couplet in the book ran as follows: "Oh, where for refuge should I flee, If Jesus had not died for me?"

At 7.30 a.m., Palmer was brought a cup of tea, and more brandy and water. He remarked that he was perfectly comfortable.

The High Sheriff, Lt. Col. Dyott, and the Under Sheriff, R.W. Hand, joined the Governor of the gaol in the condemned cell at 7.40 a.m., and they told the prisoner that the time had come for the sentence to be carried out. The hangman, George Smith, had a fearful reputation. His face was permanently fixed with a look of grim determination, and the press had reported several incidents - perhaps true, perhaps not - to add to his image. One report said that he had been in prison for running through a village naked. By trade, Smith, who lived near Dudley, was a "higgler" - an itinerant vendor - and it seems that hanging was a spare-time occupation.

There was no emotion from Palmer as his arms were pinioned, but he did ask Smith to see that the cord was not drawn too tightly before the "drop". One press report said that Palmer was so calm at this stage that it was as if he had been under the hands of a valet dressing for a dinner party!

Again the Chaplain called, in order to try to obtain a last-minute confession from Palmer. But again the prisoner was adamant, and said that his sentence was not a just one. "Then your blood be upon your own head", said the Chaplain.

In a few minutes, Palmer was brought out of his cell, and he stepped down to the basement with a jaunty stride and a smile on his face. The grim procession then formed itself. This included the Chaplain, who was reading the customary portion of the burial service; the Warders (George Plimmer and George Roberts); the head Turnkey; the Governor, Major W. Fulford; the Deputy Governor; the High Sheriff; the Under Sheriff; the Chief Constable (J.H. Hatton); the representatives of the press, and, of course, the prisoner. They all moved across the crescent yard, and past the prison hospital to the lodge. During this macabre ritual the gaol bell sounded the doom of the culprit.

The Chaplain continued to read the burial service

as the procession approached the road. It was noticed how firmly the prisoner walked along. He seemed to be the least affected of anyone in the group.

Chapter 6
The Day of Reckoning

Out in the streets of Stafford in the early morning of June 14th., 1856, crowds of people were awaiting the hour of 8 a.m. when William Palmer, often called the Prince of Poisoners, would meet his fate. All through the night it had drizzled with rain, so the public houses, which had remained open all night, were packed. To many visitors it was not too serious an occasion, though there was no general rowdyism. Here and there a party under the influence of liquor reeled out of public houses, and lapsed into drunken songs. But on the whole it was quiet until about 3.0 a.m., when daylight gradually began to appear. From now on, groups began to move towards the gaol, until the approaches to the front entrance were packed for a considerable distance.

Some of the Nonconformist chapels had remained open throughout the night for prayers and services. At the close of the services, men came forth, distributing tracts referring to the drama soon to be enacted. One such man, a Mr Ratcliffe, from Liverpool, handed out a great number of tracts and a smaller number of Bibles. Preachers were holding forth to sections of the crowd. Other men carried large placards with appropriate texts of Scripture, such as "Prepare to meet Thy God". One such placard, held by a man with long hair and a beard, was positioned near to the scaffold, in the hope that Palmer would read its message before he fell to his death. But the man was asked to move the placard before the execution took place.

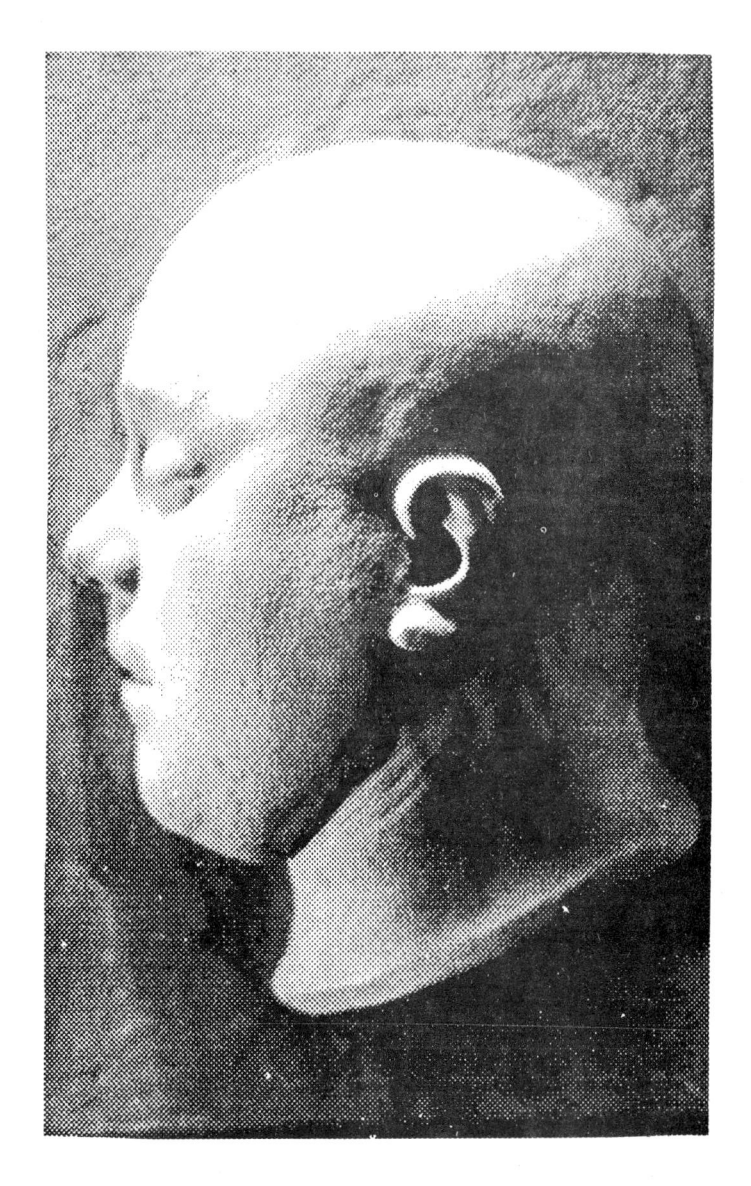

Palmer's death mask

An enormous number of spectators had gathered in the streets of Stafford. They were tired, footsore and travel-stained, but still full of anticipation about the spectacle they had come to see. Many had tramped for long distances to the town. For fully five hours, carriages of every kind, laden to extreme capacity of horses and vehicles, poured into the town in an unremitting stream, and the approaches to the gaol were jammed. On the Wolverhampton Road, the scene was the most extraordinary. From midnight to 6.0 a,m, there was a stream of carts, omnibuses - many with four horses - and all descriptions of vehicles. From the Potteries the number of vehicles was almost as numerous. All the platforms near the prison which offered specially good vantage points were soon occupied. The press reporters - about 40 in all - were nearly all in their positions by 5.0 a.m.

The railway authorities had been kept very busy, and many hundreds of people had arrived by train to stay overnight in Stafford, so that they would not miss the spectacle.

If it had not rained all night, there would undoubtedly have been a much larger crowd. As it was, between 30,000 and 40,000 people were jammed within sight of the "drop". The vast majority of these were men. Even so, some fainted in the crowd, and had to be treated.

At seven minutes to eight the prison bell tolled, to announce the departure of the procession from the cell of the condemned man. The hoarse murmur of the crowd gave way to a roar, with shouts of "Murderer!", "Poisoner!". To cries of "Hats off!" the noise subsided, and all faces were upturned as the procession approached the scaffold. Here and there a nervous laugh came from the crowd.

The scaffold was a huge affair, hung with black cloth. It was brought out in front of the prison *buildings to encroach upon the road, and thus circumscribe the points occupied by the spectators. Men had brought out this scaffold at about 4.0 a.m.*

The condemned man climbed the steps to the platform with a quick, firm step, and placed himself in the centre of the "drop" with his feet towards Gaol Square. "Is it safe?" he enquired anxiously. He wore the customary prison dress of coarse woollen jacket and trousers, with a check shirt, and was bareheaded. He was ghastly pale, but otherwise seemed unmoved, though those nearest to him said afterwards that they could see his chest heaving quickly. George Smith, the hangman, "dressed to kill" in his usual execution outfit consisting of a long white smock and a top hat, placed a rope round the prisoner's neck, and shook hands with him. Palmer is reported to have replied "God bless you!". While the Chaplain said a final prayer, Smith drew the white cap over Palmer's face with great aplomb.

It was soon over. The bolt was drawn and the "drop" fell. There were a few stifled screams from the crowd. One lady, perched high on a vantage point, was watching every movement of the prisoner through a telescope. But Palmer, a heavy man, never struggled. Only a few convulsive twitchings of his arms and legs were to be seen before his body came to rest.

The "Prince of Poisoners" had breathed his last, and his limbs now hung motionless in death.

>   *Those pinioned arms, those hands that ne'er
>   Shall be lifted again - not even in prayer.
>   That heaving breast, enough! 'tis done!
>   The bolt has fallen, the spirit gone.
>   For weal or for woe is known but to One.
>   Oh! 'twas a fearsome sight, ah me!
>   A thing to shudder at, not to see.*

FOR A FORTNIGHT.

PHOTOGRAPHIC PORTRAITS.

C. ALLEN,

Respectfully informs the Ladies, Gentry, and Inhabitants of Rugeley that he can produce

A VERY SUPERIOR PHOTOGRAPHIC PORTRAIT,

In Gilt and other Frames,

From One Shilling to One Guinea,

And solicits their patronage at the rear of the

Premises lately occupied by W. Palmer.

Specimens may be seen at Mr. James's, Bookseller.

Commencing at 10 o'Clock Mornings, until 6 in the Evenings.

RUGELEY, June 2nd, 1856.

Card of Mr Allen, Photographer

The crowd, now silent, had had their fill, and began to move away. The body was left hanging for an hour, as required by law, and was then taken away, to be covered with unslaked lime and buried without any headstone within the precincts of the prison. Before the interment, casts of the head were taken by phrenologists, who claimed to be able to read the character of a person by the nature of the bumps on his head. The death-mask of Palmer may be seen today in the Shugborough County Museum. The rope with which Palmer was hanged was made by a porter at Stafford station named Coates. With an eye to business, he made the rope thirty yards long - far too long for the execution - and cut the surplus up into short lengths, which were hawked around the crowd, usually at half a crown (12.5p.) for a two-inch piece.

After Palmer had been found guilty of poisoning John Parsons Cook, and had been sent to Stafford gaol, an enterprising photographer took over Palmer's Rugeley premises for a fortnight, offering to take a "very superior photographic portrait" of any lady or gentleman, at a cost of from one shilling to one guinea, in gilt or other frames, on the premises.

There was a persistent story - though one of uncertain authenticity - that after the Palmer hanging several local dignitaries in Rugeley, conscious of the notoriety that the Palmer case had brought to the town, decided to petition the Prime Minister of the day to see if the name of the town could be changed. They put their proposition to the Prime Minister, Palmerston, who, with a twinkle in his eye, suggested that the town should be re-named after him. After some thought, the dignitaries decided that the name of the town would be better left as Rugeley than Palmerston, for obvious reasons.

....